The LITTLE HOMES on Honey Patch

WRITTEN BY
Joy Stone

ILLUSTRATED BY
Nandina Vines

WP

WP

Published by Wilkinson Publishing Pty Ltd
ACN 006 042 173
PO Box 24135, Melbourne, VIC 3001, Australia
Ph: +61 3 9654 5446
enquiries@wilkinsonpublishing.com.au
www.wilkinsonpublishing.com.au

WilkinsonPublishing

wilkinsonpublishinghouse

WPBooks

Title: The Little Homes on Honey Patch
ISBN: 9781923259041
A catalogue record for this book is available from the National Library of Australia.

Design and Illustration by Nandina Vines.

Printed and bound in China by Asia Pacific Offset.

To Shayne,
caretaker of our nest boxes

Chapter 1

JB, aged 7, and his younger brother, **ROONEY,** nearly 4, went with Grandpa to cut down a tree for firewood.

Grandpa drove the ute down over the sandy creek crossing and up the hill to the gate of the gum tree paddock.

JB got out to open the gate.

"Leave it open," said Grandpa. "No need to close it until we come out."

"Look! Look!" called JB, pointing to the ground between two trees. "A big, big lizard."

The lizard scuttled across the dead leaves on the ground and climbed quickly up the back of a gum tree.

Rooney and Grandpa got out of the ute and came around the back of the tree to look.

"Ah," said Grandpa. "A small goanna. I have seen goannas here sometimes. This is only a young one. They can grow quite big." Grandpa stretched his arms out to show how big.

The goanna clung to the tree trunk and stayed very still.

"Keep watching him, if you like," said Grandpa. "I will look about for a tree to cut down for firewood."

"Well, you can't have that tree," said JB. "That's the goanna's tree!"

"No," said Grandpa. "I think that tree is a bit big anyway. There is a smaller one over here."

He walked a little way up the hill. JB and Rooney followed him and looked up into the branches.

"This tree has white leaves as well as green," said JB.

"The white bits are flowers," said Grandpa. "Look they are all over the tree."

"And this tree is singing," said JB. "It sings 'buzz, buzz, buzz."

"That's bees," said Grandpa. "The bees fly to the tree, creep into the flowers and get nectar.

Then they fly back to their hive and change the nectar into honey. They store the honey and use it for food."

"Here is a low branch. Watch closely. See the bees coming and going?"

"I know about bees," said Rooney. "Auntie Jo showed me bees on the flowers in her garden."

"Anyway," said JB. "We can't cut down this tree, it's the bees tree."

Grandpa pointed to a very big tree.

"I think the magpies build their nest in that one," he said. "Do you remember

getting swooped by magpies last spring?"

"We always make sure we are wearing hats when the magpies are nesting."

"Ah, the magpie's tree," said JB. "You can't cut down that one."

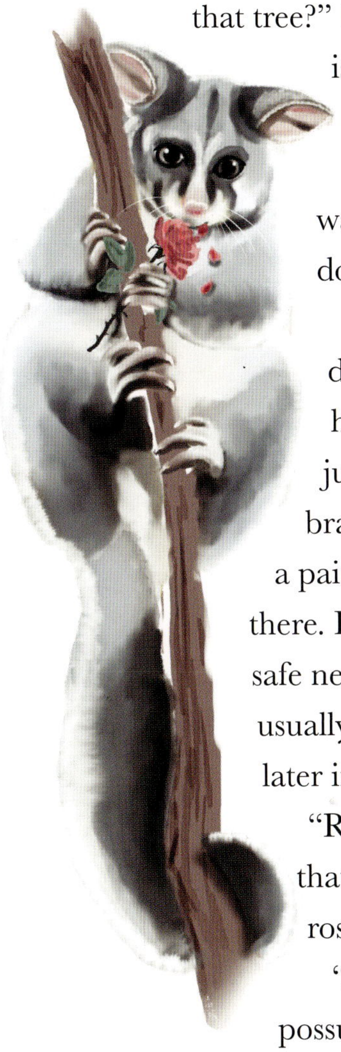

JB looked around. "What about that tree?" he said, pointing. "It is very old and nearly dead."

"No, I don't want to cut that one down," said Grandpa. "True enough it's dead, but it has a hollow in the trunk just above that second branch and every spring a pair of rosellas nest there. It must be a pretty safe nesting spot because I usually see young rosellas later in the spring."

"Right," said JB. "Not that old tree, that's the rosella's tree."

"And there are possums," said Rooney. "Nana said there are possums. Which tree do the possums live in?"

"I'm not sure where they live," said Grandpa. "But they come over to the garden at night and eat the flowers on Nana's roses. Nana said she doesn't mind too much because she likes possums."

"Once we found a dead bat on the ground near Nana's roses," said JB. "It was like a little mouse with big papery wings. Nana said it probably came from these big trees. She buried it in the garden and made us come inside and wash our hands, because sometimes bats have germs. Do you know which tree has little bats hiding?"

"No," said Grandpa. "There are probably little colonies of microbats in quite a few of the older trees. They hang upside down to sleep in the daytime and fly out at night to catch insects like mosquitoes."

"I don't like mosquitoes," said Rooney, "I hope the bats eat all of them."

"Are there koala's here?" asked JB.

"I don't think so, I have never seen one," said Grandpa. "I think koalas like different kinds of gum trees, kinds that don't grow here. These trees are mostly two sorts, called grey box and ironbark. The grey box are the ones with grey bark, and the ironbark's have very rough black bark." He pointed.

Rooney said, "There are trees like that in our street and beside the playground where we go to the swings".

"Yes," said Grandpa. "There are lots of ironbark trees in Bendigo."

"There are lots of trees here but if you keep cutting them down, soon there won't be any left." said JB.

"I don't cut down very many, maybe two or three for firewood each year," said Grandpa. "And new ones keep growing you know."

"How do new ones come?" asked Rooney.

"Well," said Grandpa. "You saw the tree with flowers. All these trees have flowers at different times in the year. And after the flowers die away, they grow into gumnuts. The gumnuts grow big and when the weather gets hotter, they split open. Inside the nuts are lots of tiny seeds and the seeds fall to the ground and get scattered about. They lie on the ground until the weather gets cooler and perhaps some rain comes along. Then some of the seeds grow little roots and little leaves and become baby trees."

"The baby trees grow bigger and bigger each year, until they are big enough to fill the spaces of any trees that have died or any trees we have cut for firewood."

Grandpa pointed to a clump of little trees at the side of the paddock. "See those young trees," he said. "They started growing in the wet spring last year. By the time you two are old enough to get your driving licences those trees will be as high as the biggest ones here.

"That's when we are 18," said JB. "That's a long time."

"Well, I'm sure this little patch of trees will still be here," said Grandpa. "Because I will always be careful not to take too many for firewood and I won't let other people take them either."

"Now I will do a deal with you two. See that tree over there. It has one stump but two trunks. I will cut one side of it down for firewood and leave the other side for the animals and birds to use."

"We'll cut it up into firewood and stack the blocks back home at the wood heap. They need to dry out for a year or two, so they burn cleanly."

"Then it will be time for lunch."

"After lunch I will make a bird nesting box for you, and we will bring it over and fasten it to the stump. You can check it out when you visit in the spring to see if any birds use it for a nest."

"That's a good deal," said JB.

"I will 'member where it is," said Rooney.

Chapter 2

GRANDPA MOVED THE ute a little bit further away, so it couldn't be hit by branches when the tree fell.

"You two get up on the back of the ute and put on your earmuffs. You must stay there while I am cutting the tree down. When it has fallen, I will tell you when it's safe to come closer."

"First, I will cut out a little bit of wood on one side, then I will make a big cut from the other side. When I have nearly cut through, the tree will groan and start to fall. I shall step back out of the way. The tree will make a great big crash when it hits the ground."

"Now you stay right here and watch!"

Grandpa took the chainsaw out of the ute. He put on his earmuffs and safety glasses.

He walked down to the tree and started the saw.

JB and Rooney held on to the rail on the back of the ute and watched.

They heard the saw motor revving.

They saw the tree start to bend over and heard it groan.

They saw Grandpa step back with the chain saw.

Then the tree was falling, falling and it hit the ground with a giant crash.

"Okay," called Grandpa. "You can come down and look now."

JB and Rooney scrambled out of the ute. They ran down to the tree and walked around it.

Grandpa brought the ute closer.

"I will cut some of the smaller branches up into blocks," he said. "Then you can help me throw them up into the ute. Stand back while I am using the saw."

JB and Rooney stood and watched while Grandpa sawed a branch into small pieces. Then when he stopped the saw, they helped to throw the wood into the ute and drag the leafy branches out of the way. Grandpa cut up another branch and then another until the back of the ute was full.

They drove back to the wood heap near the house and while JB and Grandpa stacked the wood, Rooney

HNY:PCH

ran down to tell Nana that they would soon be in for lunch.

"Nana, Grandpa is going to build a bird house and put it on the stump of the tree we cut down, so a bird can make a nest there," said Rooney.

"Is he?" said Nana. "I think I have a book about making bird nesting boxes."

She went to the big bookshelf in the lounge room and found a little book called, 'The Nestbox Book.'

Rooney sat and looked at it while Nana made sandwiches and mugs of cocoa for their lunch.

Grandpa looked at the book while he ate his lunch. "This shouldn't be too hard," he said. I've got some pieces of board in the shed. And I'll screw it to the stump so it will be nice and tight. I think we'll make the size to suit rosellas. There's a lot of them round here."

Out in the shed, JB and Rooney watched while Grandpa sawed through some old boards and screwed them together to make a box with a little lid on top. They watched while he put a special tool in his drill called a hole cutter and made a round hole like the one in the book.

Then they took the box and some screws and the drill/driver in the ute and went back to the tree they had cut down. Grandpa screwed the bottom of the box tightly on to the stump.

When they got back to the house, JB and Rooney's Mum, Sally, was there ready to take them to their home in Bendigo.

"Nana, please can I borrow this book?" asked Rooney.

"Certainly," said Nana.

Nestbox
HOLE SAW KIT

Chapter 3

AUNTIE JO, UNCLE Bruce and Big Cousin Stan lived up the hill and round a corner. Their house had a big yard, a garage and a workshop shed.

Sally sometimes stopped there to have a cuppa with Auntie Jo, after she picked up JB from school. The next time they visited, Rooney went out to the shed to talk to his Big Cousin Stan.

He told Stan how they had helped Grandpa cut firewood.

And how Grandpa had made a bird box and nailed it to the tree stump.

He showed Stan the bird box book he had borrowed from Nana.

You are good at making things out of wood," he said. "You showed me the things you made in work wood lessons at big school."

"Yes," said Stan. "Woodwork lessons."

"You made a cutting board that looks like a little pig."

"I did," said Stan.

"And you made a little sool for me to sit on," said Rooney.

"Yes, it's called a stool," agreed Stan.

"And you made a frug for Auntie Jo to pick flowers."

"Yes, it's called a trug," said Stan. "My Mum uses it when she picks flowers in the garden."

"I thought that you are so good at making things, maybe you could make some bird houses and we could get Grandpa to put them on some other trees at Honey Patch.

"Maybe," said Stan. "How many bird boxes were you thinking of?"

"One for every tree on Honey Patch," said Rooney.

"One for EVERY tree on Honey Patch? That's Hundreds!" said Stan.

"What's hundreds?" asked Rooney.

"Lots and lots!" said Stan. "I haven't got enough spare time to make that many!"

Stan thought for a minute.

"Tell you what," he said. "I'll do a deal with you; I'll make three boxes. He held up three fingers. "This many." And next time you go out to Grandpa's you can get him to put them on trees for you.

"Thank you," said Rooney.

"You will have to buy the wood," said Stan. "You better ask your mum if she will give you some money."

"Okay," said Rooney.

They went into Stan's house and found Sally and JB talking to Auntie Jo.

"Mum, I need a lot of money!" said Rooney.

"Goodness! Whatever for?"

Stan explained.

"What a lovely idea," said Auntie Jo.

"How much do you need?" asked Auntie Sally.

"About $20, I think," said Stan.

Then Auntie Jo said, "Tomorrow is Saturday. I can pick the boys up and take them shopping with Stan, to Sunny Hardware, to get the things they need for this interesting project."

"Okay" said Sally. "It's nearly time to go home and make dinner for us and our Dad."

On the way home, Rooney told JB that Stan was going to make three bird houses to put on trees at Honey Patch.

"That's great," said JB. "Can I help?"

"Yes," said Rooney.

When they got home, Rooney's Mum found an envelope, put $20 inside it and gave it to Rooney.

"Look after it carefully," she said.

Chapter 4

THE NEXT DAY, Auntie Jo took JB, Rooney and Stan in her car to Sunny Hardware.

They got a big trolley and pushed it down to the end of the store where there were lots of pieces of wood. Most of the pieces of wood were very long, but Stan found some short ones in the scrap bin, just right to make bird boxes. He put them in the trolley.

"I need some screws too," said Stan.

They pushed the trolley to shelves full of nails and screws and Stan chose a packet of long silvery ones.

Lastly, he found a hole cutting attachment to go on his power drill and checked in the nest box book to make sure it was for the right size holes.

"I think my dad has some old load binder straps in the garage," said Stan. "I can use them to make ties to fasten the boxes to trees.

"Is that all you need?" asked Auntie Jo.

"I think so, "said Stan.

"Well, while we are here, I want a couple of things," said Auntie Jo.

She pushed the trolley to the gardening section at the end of the store.

There she loaded a big bag of something called 'potting soil,' and a tiny little box full of tiny little plants called 'lettuces.'

"What are the lettuces for?" asked Rooney.

"I will plant them in my garden and when they grow big, we can eat them in salads," said Auntie Jo.

"Will the birds eat them too?" asked Rooney.

"I hope not!" said Auntie Jo.

"Maybe the birds can have the scraps," said JB.

"Yes," said Auntie Jo. "My chickens are a kind of bird, and they love lettuce scraps."

She wheeled the trolley to the checkout and paid for her potting soil and lettuces.

Stan paid for hole cutter.

Then Rooney took out his envelope and gave it to the checkout lady.

"So, you are paying for the wood and the screws," she said. "What are you going to do with them?"

"We are going to make three little houses for birds," said Rooney.

"What a lovely idea!" she said.

She opened the envelope, took out Rooney's $20 note, put it in her money box and then put a pink note and three coins back in the envelope.

"That's your change," she said.

Chapter 5

BACK AT STAN'S SHED, they unloaded the wood.

Auntie Jo gave them each a glass of her Kombucha to drink.

Kombucha was a drink Auntie Jo made, because she said it was healthier than bought drinks in cans. The boys had seen the Kombucha brewing in a big bowl on an old bench in her spare room, beside the glass bottles she used to store it when it was finished.

"Now," she said to Stan, you can walk JB and Rooney home."

"I want to start cutting out the bird boxes," said Stan, "Couldn't you take them in the car?"

"I'm not starting up the car to go just four blocks," said Auntie Jo. "Take your bike then you can get back quickly. I'll ring Sally and get her to come out the front of her house to meet you. Once you get around the corner, you'll see her and then you can leave the boys and ride back."

When Stan got back to the shed, his mate, Brad was there.

"What are you doing with all this wood?" said Brad.

"Building bird boxes," said Stan.

"What for?" asked Brad.

Stan told Brad how Rooney had watched Grandpa make a bird box and fasten it to a tree stump. He also explained how Rooney had asked him to make more bird boxes. And how Rooney had got some money from Auntie Sally, his mum, to buy the wood.

He showed Brad Nana's book.

Brad turned over the pages.

"This is cool," he said. "I could make a couple of bird boxes for Rooney. "Can I borrow this book? I will ask our woodwork teacher, Mr Robinson, if I can use some of the wood in the scrap box at school to make them. He said we could make a free choice article when we finish our projects for this term, and I've nearly finished mine."

Brad took Nana's book to the woodwork class and showed it to some of the other boys and girls there.

Most of them had finished their

projects for Term 2. They said they would like to make bird boxes for Stan's little cousin, Rooney.

Mr Robinson came over to see what the fuss was about. He held up the book to show it to the rest of the class. "You can make a bird nesting box for Rooney if you like", he said, "but you need to finish your woodwork projects first. And you will have to buy or find your own materials."

The end of class buzzer sounded. The students filed out talking about little animals and birds that might need homes.

"Wait a minute, Stan!" called Mr Robinson. "I think I might need your grandpa's phone number!"

Chapter 6

AND SO, on a sunny June day near the end of Term 2, a little school bus pulled into the Gate of 'Honey Patch'.

After it came some cars with parents to help and two utes with long ladders up on top belonging to dads who were tradies.

While the woodworkers were busy putting their boxes on trees, Auntie Sally and Auntie Jo set up a barbeque and two picnic tables near a sandy spot in the creek bed, and when everyone had finished with their boxes they came to play there in the soft sand.

Auntie Jo put some bottles of her Kombucha and two loaves of buttered sourdough bread on a picnic table. Other mums put salads and dips.

Uncle Bruce started to cook his homemade herb sausages on the barbeque.

Nana asked if any of the woodworkers would like to see some other kinds of bird nests while they waited for the sausages to cook.

She took them for a little walk and showed them a tiny nest made by Blue Wrens in a big Lavender bush.

She showed them where the swallows had made mud nests under

the eaves of the house.

She showed them where a Grey Thrush had nested in a plant pot full of leaves on a shelf in the shed.

" I especially like the Grey Thrushes, because they eat grapevine caterpillars," she said.

Then she took her little group down to a place beside the creek where there was a very high clay bank and showed them where Fairy Martins had made nests out of dobs of clay with a round space at the back and a little tunnel like the neck of a bottle for the entrance.

"I think the sausages will be cooked by now," she said and they walked back along the creek to the Picnic.

When everyone had nearly finished eating, Mr Robinson stood up and gave a big folder and a pair of binoculars to Nana.

There was a page in the folder for each bird box and each bat box. They had taken photos of the boxes, showing their numbers hanging on the trees below them and Mr Robinson had used Grandpa's computer and printer to print the pictures and put in the folder. Underneath the pictures were spaces for Nana and Grandpa to write dates and observations.

Nana said she would give it to Stan to take to woodwork class about once every month, during the spring.

"And..." she said to the Mums and Dads, "If any of you would like to drive out and check your boxes yourselves, you would be most welcome."

"We have made a roster to come out and check the boxes three times in the Spring," said Mr Robinson, "In case any pest birds or feral bees get into them, and we will

have a 'clean up' working bee in the summer to tidy them up for the following spring."

After everyone had finished eating, JB and Rooney's Dad, Brad's dad and Uncle Bruce got a wheelbarrow and collected all the dirty mugs, plates, spoons and Kombucha bottles, took them inside and washed them in Nana's kitchen.

JB, Rooney and some friends went to give the bucket of scraps to Nana's chickens.

After they tipped it into the pen, they stood watching while the chickens pecked up bits of scrap and ran away to hide and eat so the others couldn't steal their treasure.

JB opened the little door at the back of the pen and found two brown eggs in the nest.

The wash up Dad's brought back their wheelbarrow with all the clean dishes stacked on a towel and everyone collected their own.

The visitors started saying "Goodbye and Thank you," to Nana and Grandpa before getting into their little bus, utes and cars to drive home.

Just then, from across the creek, came the sound of Kookaburras laughing.

" Ho, Ho, Ho Hoo, Hoo, Hoo, Chuckle, Chuckle, Ha, Ha ,Hoo,"

"Well !, Listen to those Fellas !" said Grandpa.

"I reckon they're saying "Thank You."

Hoo, Hoo, Chuckle, Chuckle, Ha, Ha ,Hoo

Kookaburra Nesting Box

HONEY PATCH

The Little Homes on Honey Patch is not a true story, but 'Honey Patch' is a real place, a 40 acre hobby farm in Central Victoria.

I lived there for some years but have now moved to another little hobby farm close to the Whipstick Forest on the outskirts of Bendigo.

'Honey Patch' was just as described in the story. It had a 10 acre 'Gum Tree Paddock' some cleared open space for a house with surrounding garden and orchard and a truly delightful seasonal creek running through the middle.

So I used it as the backdrop for this story.

I imagined a little boy about 4 years old, curious, creative and clever, with a thoughtful and serious older brother. Then I blessed them both with a Grandpa interested in native animals, birds and vegetation and the rest of the story kind of created itself.

On this page, you can read all about the different animals and birds that lived on Honey Patch.

BEES

When it is flowering, a Gum (eucalyptus) tree is absolutely covered in blossoms. There is plenty of nectar for the common Honey Bees we see so often. But there are also many, many species of native bees, mostly quite small, which feast there as well. Most do not have 'hives' but dwell in very small colonies in holes in the ground or sheltered in spaces in mulch. The large Blue Banded bee frequented the garden at 'Honey Patch.' I am pleased that there is a current trend to place 'Bee hotels' (or tiny nest boxes for bees and insects) in gardens.

GOANNAS

I only saw a few Goannas while I lived on 'Honey Patch' Most are ground dwellers, but there is one kind which can climb trees. They are very large lizards, the ones I came across were about a metre long. They forage mostly on the forest floor finding small animals, frogs, birds and if they can get them, birds eggs.

EASTERN ROSELLAS

Eastern Rosellas are shown on the front cover of this book. There were many of them living on 'Honey Patch' and even more around the edge of the Whipstick forest where I am located now. They happily moved in to our nest boxes and don't seem upset by close people or vehicles. This area has many tall gums between open paddocks. 'Rosies' mostly seem to forage in the trees for the insects, flowers and seeds.

THRUSH

Thrushes nested in terracotta flower pots on several properties where I have lived. They seem to like the shelter of being in a shed or under a verandah. And they did feed their little ones on grapevine caterpillars which were numerous just about the time the thrush nestlings hatched.

MAGPIES

Black and white magpies abound in Victoria, in the countryside and in open spaces in towns. They forage on the ground and will learn to come to a feeding station offering meat scraps quite close to people and houses. They build untidy nests out of sticks in tall trees and BEWARE ! They are very protective of their nesting area swooping angrily down and pecking at any invader. 'Grandpa' advises the boys to wear hats in the Spring nesting season. I would advise them to wear bicycle helmets !

SEEDLINGS AND SAPLINGS

Young Eucalyptus trees grew on Honey Patch. Mostly they appeared after rainy periods and if they got a good start would grow on through the year. I removed those that appeared in my garden, orchard and the cleared patches round the house, but I left the ones along the creek and in the Gum Tree Paddock. In two years they would be higher than me.

FAIRY MARTINS

Fairy Martins, like swallows, catch insects on the wing for food. In many other places in Australia they live in large colonies, building their bottle shaped nests out of mud under banks, tank stands and bridges. On Honey Patch there were only about 10 nests built on a clay bank where a previous owner had made a dam and heavy rain had washed part of it away. I looked for them each Spring and one Spring there were none. That made me sad, but I think the Fairy Martins were cleverer than me. That December we had heavy, heavy rain, the creek flooded and the little clay bank was washed away.

SWALLOWS

Swallows built cup shaped nests out of daubs of mud under the eaves, up against the walls of the house at Honey Patch. They are untidy and it is easy to see where they are nesting by the white droppings on the ground under the nests. At Honey Patch this didn't matter as there was only a dirt path around the house but a tidy garden edge would need hosing down after the swallows left. Swallows dine on flying insects, which they catch on the wing, and it was a pleasure to watch them swooping and diving above the paddocks and orchard.

WRENS

Wrens lived in small groups in thick bushes. I would see them feeding, picking tiny insects out of the grass. On the outside of the warm North facing windows at Honey Patch, small spiders would spin webs, mostly in Autumn. In the Spring, the Wrens would pick out the spider webs and carry them away. to become lining for their tiny nests hidden in dense shrubs.

KOALAS

The little tree-dwelling animal so symbolic of Australia. I never saw Koalas on 'Honey Patch' although they were in bush I visited about 50 Kms away which had different varieties of gumtrees around a permanent stream. Koalas are marsupials which means the female rears her baby in her pouch. They eat eucalyptus leaves which are tough and require a specialised digestive system. Because their diet does not produce a lot of energy they doze frequently tucked in the fork of a tree.

BRUSHTAIL POSSUMS

No doubt there were many possums I did not see on 'Honey Patch' because they hide away during daytime and wake up to move about and forage at night. The large ones called brushtails certainly visited the garden and they did like roses. Sometimes I would be watching a rose bud, thinking I would pick it and bring it inside as soon as it opened, but morning would come and only a stem would remain.

SUGAR GLIDERS

Here, close to the Whipstick forest which surrounds the Northern side of Bendigo, my extended family were delighted to find that Sugar Gliders have moved in to at least one of their nest boxes. Sugar Gliders are very small possums about 30 cm long from nose to tail. A membrane extends from their front to back feet along the side of their body. By extending this they are able to 'glide' from tree to tree. They eat insects when available and also obtain sap by biting through the bark of trees. They live in family groups and vigorously 'defend' a territory of about a hectare around their nest.

BATS

I did not often see little bats at Honey Patch. I guess they sheltered in the bigger, older trees. Here near Bendigo they are common and I am told are often found sheltering in the roofs or walls of old buildings, apparently causing very little disturbance to the humans who live there. Little bats' bodies are about the size of mice but they look bigger with the wings spread. Each evening at dusk they fly out of their homes and spend the night catching insects on the wing. At dawn they return and sleep through the daylight hours, hanging upside down. So a bat nesting box is open at the bottom and has shade mesh or something similar on the inside walls and roof for little bat feet to grip.

KOOKABURRAS

I had a large orchard at Honey Patch. I fertilized it with compost and lots of mulch: anything I could find to cover the ground and protect the soil surface, wood chips, old hay and weeds lopped off with the brush cutter. This dense mixture protected many life forms including insects, spiders, worms, lizards, and snakes. I didn't see them very often, but I knew they were there. AND I suspected I was not the only one who knew they were there ! Kookaburras perching on the Power Line which ran along the road out front were VERY INTERESTED in that orchard!

Rosella's Home

A LIST OF THINGS YOU NEED TO BUILD ROSELLA NESTING BOX

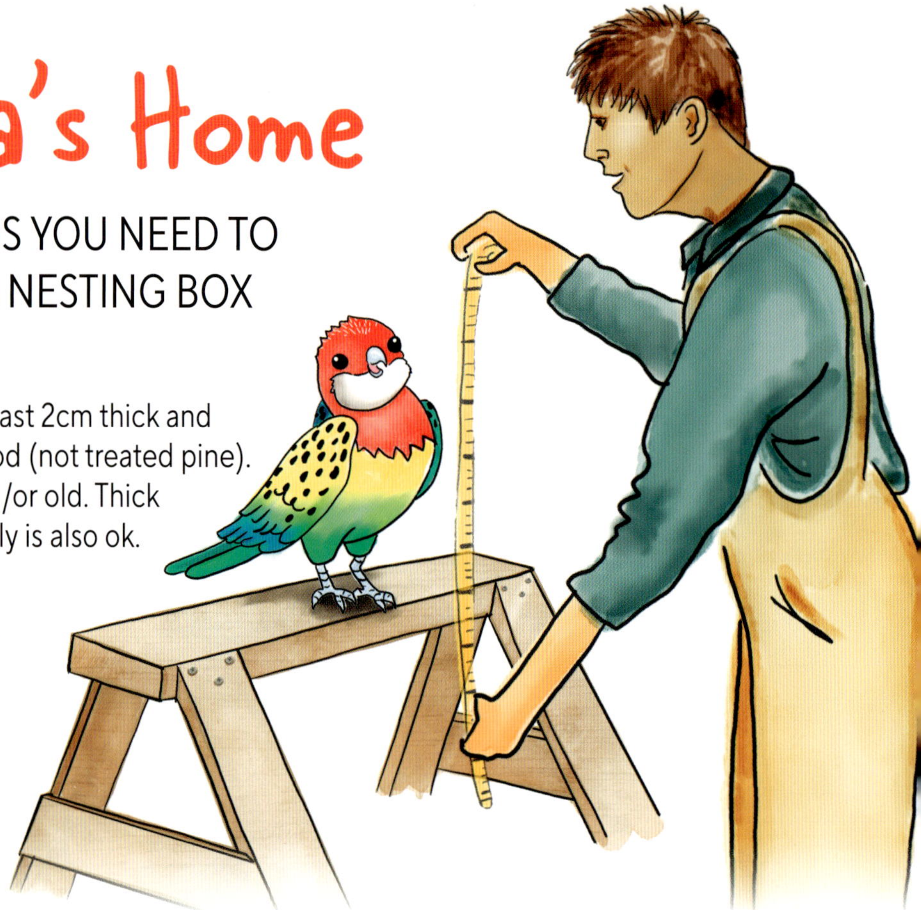

1. Wood.

Boards need to be at least 2cm thick and natural hard or soft wood (not treated pine). They can be rough and /or old. Thick exterior ply or marine ply is also ok.

2. Paint.

Not really necessary. If you do paint use water based for the outside and linseed oil inside.

3. Hinges.

You can use hinges for the lid or just simply screw it on. It is easy to undo the screws if you need to look inside.

4. The lid needs to be sloped and overhang the edges a bit so rain can run off quickly.

5. Drill 3 or 4 holes in the bottom for drainage.

6. Fasten Wire mesh or wooden slats on the inside wall between the floor and the entrance hole for the birds to use as a climbing ladder.

7. To attach to a tree, use wire covered with a piece of old garden hose, to stop it cutting in to the tree or pieces of old tie down straps. No matter if it wobbles a little bit, that's just like the wind blowing.

8. Inside put a handful of sawdust (not treated pine) or very small, dry wood chips or bark bits

9. It is not necessary to exactly follow these dimensions and directions. There are many occupied nest boxes that are bigger, smaller or have entrance holes in a different position. You might find a little box at a recycle centre that you can modify. Have a Go! Your birds will thank you !

10. Maintenance.

If you know the nest box has been occupied successfully during the nesting season there is probably no need to climb up and check it. Very old nest boxes may benefit from repainting, cleaning out the inside and repairing any holes. But the most important thing to watch for and promptly remove, is pest birds or bees.

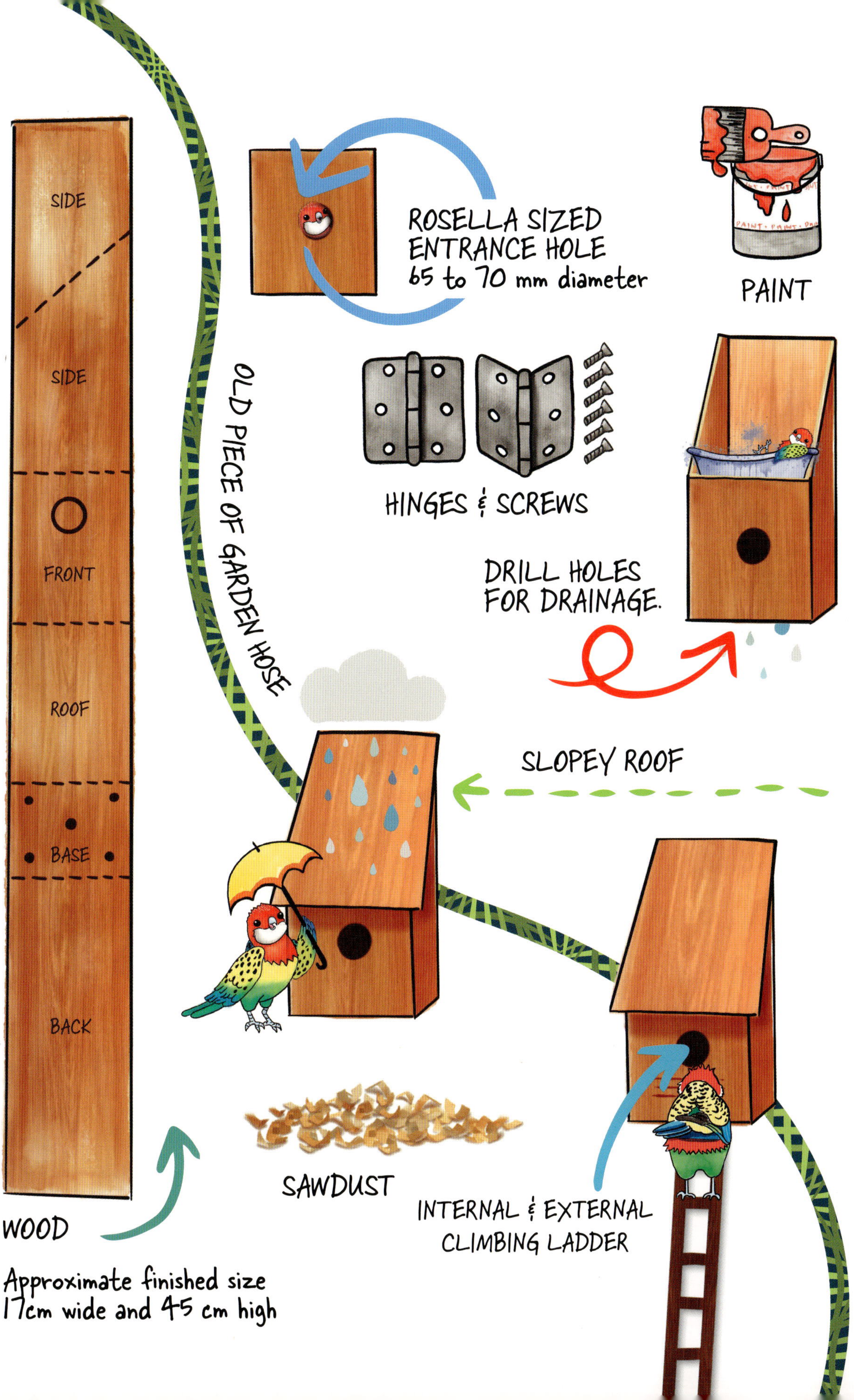

Approximate finished size
17cm wide and 45 cm high

ROSELLA'S FORTRESS

Starlings and Indian Mynas are birds which have been introduced to Australia and become pests, competing aggressively with native birds for food and nesting spaces.

It has been noticed that these birds tend to fly straight in to a nesting space but native parrots will climb, using their beak to help them, up a limb or trunk of a tree and under branches to access their nest. Possums will do this also.

So, if a 'verandah' is added to the front of a nestbox parrots readily climb under it but it frustrates mynas and starlings. Also the little entry perch needs to be attached closely to the wall under the entrance hole so that Mynas find it difficult for landing.

It is a bit difficult to work out the best distance to place the 'verandah' away from the wall of the box. Ours are about 9 cm. There has to be enough space so a Rosella can climb under but not enough that a myna can easily fly under and curve up into the entrance of the nest.

Anti Indian Myna Bird 'Verandah'
NO MYNA BIRDS ALLOWED
Mynas Keep Out!
MYNA FREE ZONE
GO AWAY MYNAS!
DO NOT ENTER MYNA BIRDS
NO ACCESS FOR MYNAS
Mynas BEWARE!
Indian Myna Birds KEEP OUT

About the Author

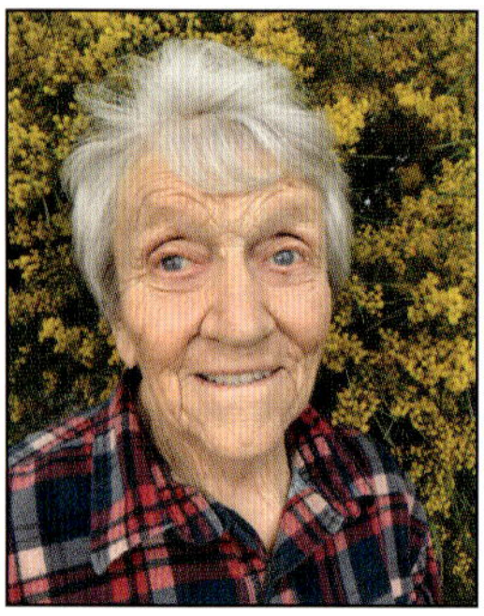

Joy has lived on the fringe of farming for most of her life. She has retired to a 20 acre hobby farm near Bendigo, which she shares with a few cows, a few chickens and a few too many heritage apple trees.

Joy is a long time member of the Weston A Price Foundation which teaches how to regain and maintain good health by eating nutrient dense foods. Also how to farm in a manner which produces nutrient dense foods. (Organic, bio dynamic, regenerative and similar natural farming systems,).

She is a short time member of Friends of the Whipstick Forest. This forest, wraps around the northern side of Bendigo. During the Gold rushes (1850's) the area was completely cleared as timber was used for supports in underground mining, fires to drive steam powered crushing machinery and many, many camp fires. So the regrown Whipstick forest is very young and not rich in old tree hollows, which might explain why those of us who live close to the forest's edge have good occupancy rates in our nest boxes.

Joy treasures living close to extended family and sharing their activities.

About the Illustrator

Nandina Vines is a passionate illustrator based in the heart of the Hunter Valley NSW, where the lush landscapes and diverse wildlife inspire her every stroke. With a keen eye for detail and a deep love for nature, Nandina specialises in bringing animals to life through her vibrant illustrations.

From whimsical bushland creatures to majestic marine life, her work captures the beauty and intricacies of the natural world. Nandina's artistic journey began in childhood, sketching the animals she encountered during her earlier life on the East Coast of Australia. Over the years, she honed her skills at university, where she developed her style.

When she's not illustrating, Nandina enjoys exploring bush walking with her dogs, acrylic painting and spending time with family. Through her art, she aims to raise awareness about the importance of preserving our planet's precious ecosystems. Nandina has illustrated many children's picture books and she continues to be inspired by animals and nature.

www.nandinavinesillustrator.com
vinesnandina@gmail.com

The
Nestbox
Book
GOULD LEAGUE